Changing the Pattern
The Story of Emily Stowe

by

Sydell Waxman

Published by
Napoleon Publishing
Toronto Ontario Canada

Napoleon Publishing gratefully acknowledges
the support of the Canada Council
toward its publishing program.

Cover design and book design by
Pamela Kinney

Printed in Canada

*To my mother, Rose Zamikoff
and all mothers, past and present – S.W.*

Canadian Cataloguing in Publication Data

Waxman, Sydell, date
        Changing the pattern : the story of Emily Stowe

ISBN 0-929141-43-1 (bound) . – ISBN 0-929141-39-3 (pbk.)

1. Stowe, Emily Howard, 1831-1903 – Juvenile
literature. 2. Women physicians – Canada – Biography –
Juvenile literature. 3. Women – Suffrage – Canada –
History – 19th century – Juvenile literature.
I. Potts, Linda, date –   . II. Title.

R464.S76W38 1995   j610'.92   C95-931598-5

Changing the Pattern

The Story of Emily Stowe

by Sydell Waxman

Illustrations by Linda Potts

Napoleon Publishing

◆ The Same Pattern ◆

When Emily Howard Jennings was born in 1831, girls' lives followed a set pattern. Some girls secretly dreamed of becoming doctors or lawyers. Others just wished for a good education. Their dreams remained empty wishes, unlikely to come true. In the Victorian age, every girl's future was limited to housework and child care.

Quilt-making gave women the rare opportunity to make choices. They picked from a rainbow of colours and threads, creating their own unique patterns.

Emily struggled to make women's lives more like quilting, something they themselves designed and directed.

Despite extreme opposition, Emily Stowe became the first woman school principal and the first woman to practise medicine in Canada. As a leader, a speaker and a fighter for women's rights, she gradually changed laws and attitudes.

How did she do it?

QUILT-MAKING

Quilt-making was women's work. Women gathered together at quilting "bees" to share stories and sewing decisions. They worked together on one large quilt or on a sampler quilt which was arranged in block form, piece by piece.

THE VICTORIAN AGE

Victoria was Queen of Britain from 1837–1901. During this period, called the Victorian age, there were strict rules about what a woman could and could not do. Most girls didn't even go to school. If her parents were rich, she went to a private school where she learned things like painting, piano playing and needlepoint.

A New Dream

Little Emily often dreamed about becoming a doctor. She watched as her mother Hannah and other Quaker women prepared medicine for their families. When she was old enough, she applied to the Toronto School of Medicine.

Emily's application shocked the University Senate. All doctors at that time were men. Since a woman had never applied for medical courses, the Senate didn't know what to do. Her papers were sent to John McCaul, President of the University of Toronto. McCaul was annoyed with Emily, but agreed to discuss her application.

As Emily guided her horse and carriage to the front of the huge university building, her heart kept pace with the heavy clopping of her horse's hooves. Could the men on the Senate do something that had never been done before? Would they accept a woman into the university?

In his office, McCaul spoke sternly. Her case, he said, had been debated for a long time. The Senate had reached a decision. Women were not allowed.

Emily breathed quickly. This was unfair. "Why?" she asked. McCaul answered that boys were used to studying with other boys. Girls belonged at home.

The Promise

DR. "JAMES" MIRANDA STUART BARRY

There was one female doctor in Canada before Emily. For 46 years, Miranda Barry dressed as a man and called herself "James" Barry. When she was Inspector-General of Military Hospitals in Canada from 1857–1861 no one guessed she was a woman. Her secret was discovered after she died and her body was being prepared for burial. Many people told Emily to copy Miranda, but Emily wanted women to be accepted as themselves.

Emily was a short woman, but she jolted upright and stood stiffly before this powerful man. "Your Senate may refuse to admit women now, but the day will come when these doors will swing wide open to every female who chooses to apply."

McCaul was not impressed with Emily's boldness. "Never in my day, Madam. The doors of the University are not open to women and I trust they never will be."

Emily vowed, "Then I will make it the business of my life to see that they will be opened, that women may have the same opportunities as men."

Emily never forgot this promise. But before she could change the lives of all Canadian girls, she had to struggle to change her own future, by adding pattern pieces to her own life.

Where did she get the courage?

Society Of Friends

QUAKERS

The Quakers are a religious group founded over 300 years ago in England by George Fox. They called themselves The Society of Friends, but other people called them Quakers because they "shook" with emotion at their meetings. Like all Quakers, Emily's family called each other "friend" or "brother" and used the words "thee" and "thou."

SILENT MEETINGS

At the Quakers' meeting house, the elders sat on a raised platform. There was no leader, so the Quakers prayed in silence. If someone felt the need to express an idea, he or she just spoke out. The meeting was over when no one had any more comments.

When Emily was born in 1831, her parents, Hannah and Solomon Jennings, were just as happy to have a girl baby as a boy. Like all Quakers, they believed that every person's soul contained the seed of God. The Quakers were the first religious group to accept women as equals.

In her town, called Norwich, a Quaker farming community west of Toronto, Emily saw Quaker women become ministers. She watched as women stood and spoke freely at Quaker meetings.

Emily didn't know that the rest of Canada had rigid ideas about girls' education and work. At home, on the farm, everyone shared the never-ending chores.

Work That's Never Done

QUAKER DRESS

Women wore simple dresses with long sleeves. Ruffles, edging or decorations were not allowed. Men wore broad-brimmed hats. The women wore colourless "coal-scuttle" muslin bonnets. The Quakers' dark, plain clothes represented the plain life they lived.

GIRLS DO WOMEN'S WORK

Even little girls worked all day. A ten year-old girl might be expected to do a large washing, spin yarn for hours, bake 20 loaves of bread and weave, all in one day.

Emily learned how to make butter, candles, soap and ink. She shared all the daily jobs with her five younger sisters, Cornelia, Paulina, Hannah, Ethlinda and Ella. In the evenings, they sewed their own calico clothes by hand.

Much of their summer was spent preparing food and clothing for winter. The Jennings filled their barn with hay and grain. Then they picked potatoes and carrots, stocking their root cellar for the winter.

Dressed in their dark Quaker clothes, even in the heat of late summer, Emily and her family preserved fruits and vegetables.

Emily couldn't wait for the routine chores to end so she could go with her mother to her favourite place. Filled with bright reds and yellows, with plants above the ground and edible roots below, the garden smelled of sweet herbs.

Her mother's special herb garden was probably the place where Emily first dreamed of becoming a doctor.

Hannah's Garden

HANNAH JENNINGS

Hannah had been educated at a Quaker boarding school in the United States. She returned to Norwich and married Solomon Jennings. Emily was the eldest of her six daughters. Hannah always prepared medicines and helped the sick.

CATNIP AND COLDS

Hannah grew herbs and roots in her garden. She dried the herbs by hanging them in bunches all over the kitchen. She spread catnip plants on newspapers and left them on the porch to dry. Then she brewed catnip tea to cure colds.

Hannah Jennings, Emily's mother, transformed plants from her beautiful garden into cooking spices and healing remedies.

When a family member got sick, Hannah went to her cupboard. She selected specific herbs and mixed her own homemade medicines. Most women in the 1800's acted as the family doctor.

One day, Cornelia, Emily's sister, had a bad cold. Hannah taught Emily how to prepare catnip tea. Since they didn't have hot water bottles, Hannah heated a soapstone and put it in the bed. Soon Cornelia stopped sneezing and went back to her daily chores.

Doses,
Small and Large

**WORM-WOOD AND
BELLY ACHES**

Sometimes Hannah used peppermint or ginger to cure nausea. For an upset stomach she used worm-wood, a bitter herb, which she prepared in hot water and then cooled. Emily thought it looked and tasted terrible.

The Jennings often visited their friend Dr. Joseph Lancaster (1818-1884). Emily's eyes opened wide listening to him talk about homeopathy, a new kind of medicine. Homeopaths believed in using small doses of remedies that produced the same symptoms as the illness. "Like cures like" said Dr. Lancaster and Emily remembered how Hannah used bee pollen for bee stings and hot compresses for burns. Many of her mother's treatments were similar to homeopathic cures.

Working with her mother made Emily feel strong and capable. The fragrant plants and the image of women as healers stayed like pattern pieces in Emily's mind. But Emily wasn't just collecting pleasant memories from her family. She was watching and learning about courage, something she would need in large doses.

Changing the pattern of Canadian girls' lives required a special kind of bravery.

Hiding the Rebels

THE REBELLION OF 1837

In 1837, Canada was still part of the British Empire. The Queen's representative in Canada was the Governor-General. He ruled the country and made laws. The people were upset because the Governor wasn't listening to their needs. William Lyon Mackenzie, a newspaper editor in Toronto, decided to take action. His followers, the reformers, were labelled rebels by the government. They took up arms against the government. The rebellion was short-lived, but caused the Queen to send a new Governor-General.

Emily was six during the Rebellion of 1837. She overheard Quakers talking about aiding the reformers, fighters who wanted to change the way the government was run. Peace-loving people, the Quakers wouldn't use guns, but they found other ways to help. Emily watched as those she loved risked their own lives for the rebellion.

Emily's great-uncle was a magistrate, so at first he acted as a spokesperson for the reformers. Then he gave the outlaws pork and flour. Other Quakers, including Emily's grandmother Paulina and Dr. Lancaster, hid reformers in their barns and houses.

This made the government furious. The leaders organized a citizen-army, called a militia, and sent it to Norwich to find the rebels. The government gave orders to arrest not only the rebels, but also the people who hid them.

The militia, an odd-looking army of ordinary men shaking pitchforks and guns, marched into Norwich. Although they looked more like a group of duck hunters than an army, Emily and her family quivered with fear when they heard about Great-uncle's arrest.

NORWICH

Norwich was a farming town with fertile, rolling hills and forests filled with maple and oak trees. When Emily was born it was practically a wilderness. Peter Lossing, Emily's great-grandfather, was one of the earliest settlers in the Norwich area. He had arrived in 1809 and purchased 15,000 acres for fifty cents an acre.

Courage in the Family

Emily's great-uncle was charged with high treason and, if found guilty, would be hanged. Dr. Lancaster was put in a dirty, damp jail and given little food. Emily worried about her great-uncle and kind Dr. Lancaster. She knew that Grandma Paulina was in danger as well and could be imprisoned for hiding a reformer.

Then the militia came to Emily's house. They banged on the door so hard that the hinges broke. They tramped through her house, shouting, while they looked for rebels, but they didn't find any. Emily glared through her window, her heart thumping, as the militia stomped over the rolling fields to Grandma Paulina's.

Emily didn't see this brave old woman challenge the citizen army, but later she heard Grandma tell the story of how, cool and fearless, she'd said to them, "Come in and look!" The army never found Grandma's rebel.

Changes

POEM

written in 1837 by Hanna Palmer
Moore, a Quaker

Come friends and neighbours,
pray give ear
While I relate a story
Of what took place in the first year
Of the reign of Queen Victoria
In Canada a strife began
A wild seditious frenzy
Spread by a bold ambitious man
Called William L. Mackenzie.

Because the Quakers had helped the
reformers, everyone in the village suffered.
One young Norwich rebel was hanged and
his body brought back to the village.

The Quakers had to give up their carriages
to the militia. Many villagers hid their
horses, wagons and food so the army
couldn't steal their supplies. Emily and her
family had to walk to and from meetings.
The trip was long and tiring for a six year-
old, but Emily didn't complain. She knew she
had to be strong, just like the rest of her
family.

Finally, with the help of a new Governor-
General, the laws started to change for the
better. Emily's great-uncle was found
innocent and the rebels were pardoned. Dr.
Lancaster, like so many reformers, had
escaped to the United States for awhile. He
was welcomed back home when the
reformers were no longer considered
enemies.

Willing to Die

Emily would always remember the story of Grandma hiding the rebel and Great-uncle going to jail. She'd learned that even the government, with its power and laws, could be challenged.

Her family had been willing to die for their beliefs. Someday, she too would stand up for what she believed. Someday, when it was her turn, she too would be courageous.

Back to Normal

SAMPLERS

Mothers taught daughters how to embroider the alphabet or poems onto a piece of linen or canvas. These sewn pictures became known as samplers. Girls often as young as six made samplers as a way of learning to read while practising their stitches. This is a picture of Emily's sampler.

Emily and her family relaxed and rejoiced. Life in Norwich went back to normal.

Normal meant a lot of work. Emily and Cornelia, her sister who was two years younger, shared many jobs. They milked cows, churned butter and baked bread. Sitting around the fireplace, the girls sewed samplers with neat even stitches. They knitted undershirts for winter. Then they quilted covers from rags and old clothing, perhaps wishing their choice of futures was as plentiful as their colourful threads.

In 1844, when Emily was thirteen years-old, Hannah encouraged the girls to make baby clothing, a small quilt and some rag toys.

Baby Brother

A midwife, a woman who delivered babies, came to Emily's house in April. Since babies were born at home, Emily may have boiled water or held her mother's hand. Finally, Hannah gave birth to a baby boy. Emily, being the oldest, fed and cuddled baby John.

During the 1800's, hundreds of children under the age of five died. Epidemics of typhoid, influenza and the dreaded cholera spread rapidly. People didn't know that germs, cleanliness and disease were connected. The water was often unclean and milk wasn't pasteurized. Like so many other babies, John died when he was only five months old.

Emily saw John's tiny coffin being buried. Why did baby John have to die? Someday, she resolved, when she became a doctor, she would help children live.

EPIDEMICS

Epidemics, illnesses which affected hundreds of people, spread very quickly in the 1800's. An epidemic of cholera or typhoid left thousands, including many children, dead. A cemetery in the 1800's had many small tombstones decorated with inscriptions.

In Loving Memory of John Jennings 1844

Home Is School

CANDLESTICKS

Emily and her sisters had to do their school work at night, even though there were no lights. A wax candle was often pushed into a slice of potato to make a candlestick.

All the farm work and baby John's tragic death didn't stop Hannah from educating her girls. The schools in the area were often run by fourteen or fifteen year-olds with no special training. Since Hannah had been educated at an American Quaker school, she decided to give her children lessons at home.

Using scratchy ink pens and flickering candlelight, Hannah taught her six girls everything she knew. Emily also acted as a teacher for her younger sisters Cornelia, Paulina, Hannah, Ethlinda and Ella.

Neighbours noticed and admired Emily's intelligence and hard work.

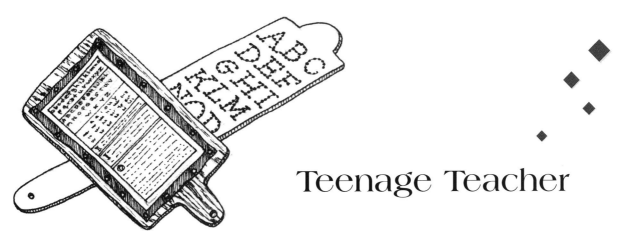

Teenage Teacher

HORNBOOKS

Up until the early 1800's, children learned the alphabet, the nine digits and the Lord's Prayer from hornbooks, pieces of wood that looked like paddles. Letters were either printed on a card or carved into the wood. Then a clear, thin piece of horn was placed over the alphabet. When Emily was a teacher, hornbooks were already rare. Today finding a hornbook is like finding a treasure.

TEACHING

During the 1840's there weren't enough male teachers, so the school boards started to hire women. Many people complained. Each board had to limit the number of women hired. Young girls like Emily, aged fourteen or fifteen, were lucky to be chosen.

When Emily was fifteen, Dr. Ephraim Cook, the township's Superintendent of Education, chose her to teach in Summerville, a town close by. For girls in 1846, teaching was the only acceptable job outside the home. Emily felt honoured, even though teaching meant she had to leave home and stay with strangers. She missed her sisters, especially Cornelia, but she didn't have time to worry about being lonely.

Not only was Emily hired to teach all the grades, but she also had to clean the school and keep the fire going in winter. Her students helped by bringing logs to school.

School hours were from nine to three. At half past twelve, Emily rang a bell and all the children rushed around, opening lunch tins and stuffing themselves. When Emily opened her tin box, she often found a dish, a few thin slices of meat, a piece of bread, a cup of cream and a raw egg. She threw the egg into the fire until she heard a popping sound. Then she peeled off the burnt egg shell and ate the hot centre.

Emily taught her pupils reading, writing, simple arithmetic, geography and English grammar. Like other teachers, she had a Bible, a speller, a reader and an arithmetic book. She may have been one of the fortunate teachers who also owned a history or geography book.

One-Room Schoolhouse

NEW LAW

In 1871, Canada passed a law forcing children ages 7 – 12 to attend school for at least four months of every year.

Facing the class from a raised platform at the front, Emily's strong, clear voice filled the room. She gave each student a small, black slate board. The pupils memorized their work before brushing it off.

Most of Emily's students came to school for just a few months since their help was needed on the farms. This meant her pupils were of different ages. Some of the older boys were bigger than Emily, but she didn't let this bother her.

What did annoy her was that she was paid half the salary of a male teacher, although she was doing the same work. She also knew that she would have to stop work if she got married.

Despite these disadvantages, Emily loved teaching. New thoughts and facts danced in her mind, making her realize she wanted more knowledge and further education. Where could Emily go for a higher education?

Wanting More

She applied to Victoria College in Cobourg, but was told that women were not accepted.

There was one school that Emily could attend. All she needed was enough money and she could go to the Normal School in Toronto, a new college that trained teachers.

Emily taught for six years to save money for teachers' college. In 1853, when she was 22 years old, she was finally ready to set out for Toronto. She said good-bye to her family and prepared to travel for six hours by carriage along the dirt road. Listening to the rhythmic clopping of the horse's hooves, Emily wondered what lay ahead. What would a bustling city like Toronto look like?

SALARY

In 1858, women teachers earned less than half the amount of a male teacher. The average wage for a woman was $170.00 a year, while a man earned $520.00.

Toronto, 1868

The Big City

In 1853, Toronto had 35,000 people and big buildings like the Normal School. Everywhere, horses and wagons seemed to mingle with people going in all directions.

People stared at Emily, pointing at her plain, dark Quaker clothes and her simple bonnet. She stared back at all the colourful dresses, the stores and the busy, noisy streets.

She hoped to find a Quaker meeting house, but there was none. Luckily, she was comfortable with Methodists since they had also lived in Norwich. Later in life, she became a Methodist.

Regularly, she bought *The Globe*, Toronto's newspaper, owned by George Brown. She had never read such a large, interesting paper. Papers were especially important in Emily's time because there were no radios or televisions.

She didn't know that someday her name would appear in *The Globe.* She didn't know that she was to become one of Canada's most important, controversial women.

Questions

EGERTON RYERSON

Ryerson signed Emily's Teacher's Certificate. In 1844, he had been appointed Superintendent of Education in Upper Canada. Ryerson believed in a useful, practical education. Although he was progressive in many areas, Ryerson still held Victorian views on the role of women. He thought that a university education was a waste of time, because it wouldn't make women better mothers.

Behind the Normal School was a model class used by the student teachers to practise lessons. A long hall separated the two buildings. The women had to walk on one side of the hall and the men on the other. They were not allowed to speak to one another in class. Emily didn't understand the reason for this separation. Men and women in Norwich had talked and walked together.

All kinds of questions formed in Emily's mind. Why were women not allowed into university? Why had she earned less money than a man? Why did she have to walk on the other side of the hall?

Training in Normal School lasted six months. She started school in November and graduated in May 1854, proving by her exceptional marks that she deserved a First Class Teacher's Certificate.

NORMAL SCHOOL

The Normal School, a training place for teachers, was built in 1852. This large school took up an entire city block on Gould Street in Toronto.

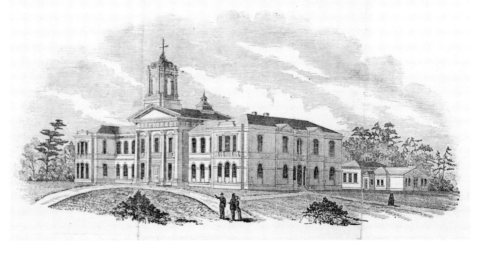

RULES FOR TEACHERS
1872

1. Teachers each day will fill lamps, clean chimneys and trim candles.

2. Each teacher will bring a bucket of water and a scuttle of coal for the day's session.

3. Make your pens carefully. You may whittle nibs to the individual tastes of the pupils.

4. Men teachers may take one evening each week for courting purposes, or two evenings a week if they go to Church regularly.

5. After ten hours in school the teachers should spend their remaining time reading the Bible or other good books.

6. Women teachers who marry or engage in uncomely conduct will be dismissed.

7. Every teacher should lay aside from each pay a goodly sum of his earnings for his benefit during his declining years so that he will not become a burden on society.

8. Any teacher who smokes, uses liquor, frequents pool or public halls, or gets shaved in a barbershop will give good reason to suspect his worth, intentions, integrity and honesty.

9. The teacher who performs his labours faithfully and without fault for five years will be given an increase of 25 cents per week in his pay providing the Board of Education approves.

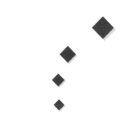

First Woman Principal

Emily had graduated with marks so high that a school in Brantford hired her, not as a teacher, but as their principal. Brantford had just built a new school and perhaps they hired Emily because they could pay her less than a man.

Emily was not one to turn down an opportunity. At age 23, Emily Jennings became the first woman principal in Canada. (Ontario was still known as Canada West in 1854.)

Some of the parents didn't approve of a woman principal and the children would giggle and whisper behind her back. Emily never worried about what others thought. She found the scene from her school window comforting with its familiar large oak trees, and she just went on with her work. Brantford was in a beautiful part of the country, not far from Norwich and near Mount Pleasant where she worshipped as a Methodist.

John Stowe, a carriage-maker and lay preacher, often walked her home from church.

The Man With The Octagon House

OCTAGON HOUSES

Around 1850, John Stowe built several eight-sided houses. Many believed that the octagon shape brought peace and tranquillity.

A central furnace or stove made heating easier.

A central skylight brought sunshine into all the rooms. Emily's house had several levels with John's carriage shop on the ground floor. Horses and wagons lined the front of her house. The banging and building sounds mingled with the horses' neighing so that it was seldom quiet at the Stowe's house.

One day after church, John took Emily to see his special house. Emily had never seen anything like John Stowe's unique home — a house with eight sides. John showed Emily how his father had built the house so that his carriage-making shop was downstairs while his family lived upstairs. Emily must have liked this strange house, but, even more important, she liked John Stowe.

Born in England, John had come to Canada at the age of thirteen. He immediately started working with his family as a carriage-maker.

When Emily and John married on November 22, 1856, John's family built an octagon house in Mount Pleasant — for Emily.

A friend described John as, "a liberal-minded man whose brilliant wife could always count upon him for sympathy and assistance." John was an understanding person who accepted new ideas and encouraged Emily throughout her long struggle.

John set up his business downstairs and Emily retired from school to raise a family. All women were expected to stop teaching when they got married.

21

Women's Work

Carriage-making prospered since everyone needed horses and wagons for travelling. As well, John built sleds for the winter. Emily seemed happy as a homemaker, but probably, like so many people of her time, didn't talk about her feelings.

Once a visitor tasted Emily's pie and said that he'd rather see a woman bake delicious pies than get an education. Emily answered that she could handle both tasks.

Even though Emily thought women should have the right to an education and career choices just like men, she still believed that homemaking and child care were valuable jobs.

BATH

Bath time took hours. First the candles or oil lamps were set up. Then a big tin tub was brought into the kitchen and a screen placed in front of the kitchen stove or fire. The oven, if there was one, was left open for warmth. Then the water was heated and poured into the tub. Emily liked being first because others in the family often used the same water. Afterwards, it was a chilly trip up the stairs, holding a candle to light the dark stairwell. By the end of the 19th century, many people were bathing at least once a week.

No Chains

COOKING

Emily liked to cook and entertain. She always felt that homemaking was an important job. One recipe looked like this:

Apple Pudding

"Fill a dish with apples nicely sliced, sweeten them, add spices, nutmeg, a little lemon or vanilla and cover with a crust.
Crust: one quart flour, three teaspoons baking powder, piece of butter size of an egg, salt and milk enough to mix soft dough.
Set on top of the stove until the crust rises, then bake a nice brown."

Later in 1889 Emily lectured on the importance of homemaking. These are her words:
"I believe homemaking, of all occupations that fall to woman's lot, the one most important and far-reaching in its effects upon humanity, but I would have her as free to choose her vocation as her brother man. She should be tethered by no conventionalities, enslaved by no chains either of her own or man's forging."

Remembering Remedies

TB

Tuberculosis, often called TB, consumption or the white plague was the most dreaded killer of the 1800's. It destroyed and disabled more people than any other disease in history. When John got sick, sanatoriums (places where patients went to receive fresh air and rest) didn't exist.

As Emily's family grew, she devoted herself to cooking, cleaning and child care. Augusta was born in 1857, John Howard in 1861 and Frank in 1863. Having lived on a farm, she was used to getting up early and handling lots of work.

The children went to a private school owned by their good friend, Dr. William Nelles. Nelles' Academy was also an octagon shape and may have been built by John and his family.

What did Emily do when the children got sick? That's when she thought about Hannah, the wonderful garden, the remedies and the visits to Dr. Lancaster. She brewed the catnip tea and thought about women doctors again. The children's illnesses didn't change Emily's life, but John's sickness did. In 1864, he contracted tuberculosis.

John Stowe, Emily's husband

The Killer

Tuberculosis is a deadly disease of the lungs. Doctors struggled to understand its cause and treatment. Patients were put in dark rooms. They were wrapped in ice cold blankets to ward off the fever and given little to eat. Thousands died.

Emily feared the children would catch the illness, so she discussed John's treatment with her Norwich friend, Dr. Joseph Lancaster, who believed in homeopathy. They agreed it was best for John to move away.

Somehow, Emily found the right treatment of fresh air and rest for John, likely in the country. Ten years passed before he recovered and rejoined his family. John was never again strong enough to make carriages.

While John recuperated, Emily's house was strangely quiet. She could no longer hear the sounds of the busy carriage-maker, banging and building below. She could no longer receive the benefit of John's work. Emily and her children were alone and very poor.

Emily needed a job.

SICK CHILDREN

Thousands of children died from tuberculosis. Then, in 1883, a special hospital called the Lakeside Home for Little Children was set up on Toronto Island. With fresh air and rest, many children survived.

Cornelia Jennings
Emily's sister

A REMARKABLE SISTER

Cornelia, Emily's sister, was a special person. After staying with Emily's children so Emily could study medicine, she married and travelled all over Europe. People stared at her in her modest Quaker clothes, but their whispers didn't stop Cornelia from doing what she wanted. Cornelia collected items from all over the world for an American gallery.

An Unusual Job

More and more Emily realized how unfair the laws were for women. Women couldn't own land or businesses. When they got married, everything, even their own children and any money they earned, belonged to their husbands. The husband, when he died, willed his land to his son, never a daughter or wife. Married women didn't teach. What happened if a husband, like John, got sick? She believed women needed careers just like men.

Although it was unusual for a married woman to teach, Dr. Nelles, Emily's friend and owner of Nelles Academy, gave her a job. The children were happy when Aunt Cornelia, Emily's sister, came to live with them.

The Fight Begins

CORNERSTONES

Historical papers, with information about the time period, were often placed like a time capsule into a stone. This stone was then put permanently into the corner of a new building. Records of the Nelles Academy were included in the cornerstone of the red brick school that replaced the Academy in 1911 in Mount Pleasant.

So, each morning, Emily left her sister Cornelia with the babies and took Augusta, her daughter, to the octagon school where she taught all day.

Now that she was alone with her children and had to support a family, she was more determined than ever. Emily's fight was just beginning. The pattern that had been set for her life was too confining for her abilities. Why did every woman have to do the same job, regardless of her personality, intelligence, capabilities or creativity? Emily wanted to be a doctor.

She applied to the University of Toronto. Her application was refused. Women were still not allowed.

Octagon school in Mt. Pleasant around 1880.

A SCHOOL FOR WOMEN DOCTORS

In 1850, the Quakers of Pennsylvania opened the first Woman's Medical College. Emily chose not to go to this college because she wanted to become a homeopathic doctor.

NEW YORK

If Toronto had seemed big, New York was massive. In 1865 the population was 1,300,000 and, for the first time, Emily encountered crowds of people. Immigrants from all over the world streamed from huge boats onto the busy streets.

Far From Home

There were no Canadian women for Emily to copy, so she turned to the United States where there were a few women doctors and women's colleges. Not only could Emily study in the United States, she even had a choice of three schools.

She chose The New York Medical College for Women because it taught homeopathic remedies, ones she remembered from her mother and Dr. Lancaster.

The train trip from Toronto to New York was a long, jostling and lonely ride. Of course, she knew Cornelia would take good care of her children, but all the way there she thought about how painful it felt leaving her family and taking this step into an unknown future.

28

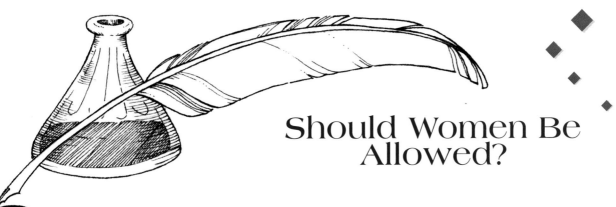

Should Women Be Allowed?

ELIZABETH BLACKWELL

Elizabeth Blackwell, the first woman in the United States to become a doctor, was allowed into medical school as a joke. The students thought it was funny when they voted in favour of Elizabeth becoming a medical student.

Afterwards, visitors came to the lectures to see this strange, "dreadful" young woman studying medicine. As soon as she graduated, the school passed a law stating that no other woman could attend.

While Emily studied medicine with other women, *The New York Times*, the main American newspaper, asked, "Should women be allowed to become doctors?" One writer thought it would be too upsetting for a lady to be a doctor. Other people thought women weren't capable of learning complicated subjects. One writer called herself "Mother Of The Old School" and wrote that women medical students were asking for insults.

Emily wondered why *The New York Times* always discussed what women should be allowed to do. Why was the question never "Should men be allowed?" Emily took out her quill and dipped and dipped until she had a long letter for the paper. This is part of what Emily wrote:

"That God has given to man more judgement, skill, talent or tact than He has seen fit to dispense unto woman, we do not believe nor acknowledge – the difference existing is entirely the result of and dependent upon their hitherto widely differing course of education. I conclude the subject in the earnest conviction that the day will yet dawn when woman will equal man, not only in the medical profession but in every other position in which she is qualified to excel."

STETHOSCOPE

René Laënnec, a French physician (1781-1826), invented the stethoscope. The first stethoscopes were rolled-up cardboard, but they allowed the doctor to hear the sounds inside the body. Later this instrument became a foot-long tube. The doctor placed one end on his ear and the other bell-shaped end onto the patient's chest. Many physicians around Emily's time carried a stethoscope in their tall, black top hats.

Stepping Outside the Sphere

Emily got used to the papers detailing women's work, which became known as "women's sphere." Any woman who dared to move outside the sphere was criticized as if she had committed a terrible crime. By studying medicine, Emily was stepping outside the sphere. Emily knew she had to fight against this popular attitude that women's work was prearranged. Women should be able to choose.

She hardened herself to deal with the whispers and laughter as she and her friends made their way to school. People along her daily route stared with puzzled, disapproving faces. They couldn't figure Emily out. What kind of human was she? Sometimes Emily wanted to laugh at their reactions, but she controlled herself.

Emily disciplined herself to be in control of her feelings, even when it came to the difficult aspects of medicine such as dissection. To gain control, Emily decided to practise cutting open an insect at home. Having pinned the insect down, she took out a pen knife. She waited with the knife poised above the dark beetle. Her stomach rolled over and she felt nauseous. She couldn't do it.

The First Cut

HORRORS

The students called the dissecting room the "chamber of horrors." It was there that the young doctors-to-be cut up dead bodies (called cadavers). Sometimes they gave the body a nickname. Dissecting, Emily discovered, was not as bad as she had thought. She was even able to eat dinner afterwards.

For a long, long time, Emily couldn't bring herself to cut the insect. Finally she relaxed and opened the insect. Practising helped. She went to her dissection classes and never again felt that initial sickness and disgust.

Emily was often tired after her long days at Medical School. She had to get up early and dissect until 9 o'clock. Then she listened to lectures, went back to the dissecting room and then home for dinner. After dinner she studied her notes, read books or wrote letters. Somehow, she even found time to meet new people.

New Friends
New Ideas

Emily's new friends, Elizabeth Cady Stanton, Lucretia Mott and Susan Anthony, were courageous women who had already started to change the pattern of girls' lives in the United States.

Not only did they agree with Emily that girls should be allowed into university and medical school, but they had also started to work for another cause – the vote for women. These women working for the right to vote called themselves suffragists.

Elizabeth Cady Stanton and Lucretia Mott had always cared about the rights of other people. In 1840, they had attended the World Anti-Slavery Convention in London, England.

The long trip by boat had been uncomfortable, but they were glad to be at the convention, fighting against slavery, alongside other people who believed in fairness.

ELIZABETH CADY STANTON

Elizabeth Cady Stanton lived in the United States. She was the first person to suggest that women be allowed to vote. This is what she said in one of her speeches:

"We ask for all you have asked for yourselves... that the rights of every human being are the same and identical."

Most people in the 1800's found Elizabeth's ideas outrageous. Not Emily.

Insulted

The male leaders fighting against slavery would not allow women to take part in the meetings. Emily's friends were insulted when they were made to sit apart at the meetings. They were allowed to listen but not to speak.

The two women came home, tired from a long, unhappy journey, yet filled with determination. In 1848, they organized the first women's meeting in the United States. Women gathered together at Seneca Falls, New York, to discuss their rights and women's sphere.

Newspapers called the gathering the "most shocking and unnatural incident ever recorded." The idea of women voting was considered scandalous.

By the time Emily graduated as a doctor in 1867, she thought, not only that women should be allowed into universities, but that women should have the right to vote.

Practice At Last

THE BLACK BAG

Emily travelled in her horse-drawn wagon with her doctor's bag at her side. Doctors carried a black bag in which they kept a thermometer, a tongue depressor and a few other simple instruments. They visited patients in their own homes, where one room was often turned into a "sick room." If unable to pay the doctor, a patient would offer something in return. This was called bartering or trading. Sometimes Emily went home with a live turkey instead of money.

MRS. DR. STOWE,
Graduate of N.Y. Medical College for Women

May be consulted in all diseases of Women and Children,

From 9 A.M. Till 3 P.M.
At No.. 26 Shuter Street.

Toronto, June 18, 1867

In the spring of 1867, the year of Confederation, Emily Howard Stowe, 36 years of age, became Canada's first practising female physician. She opened up her office at 26 Shuter Street in Toronto and advertised in *The Globe* on June 18, 1867.

Since there had never been a woman doctor, she didn't know what to call herself. The ad read: MRS. DR. STOWE. By the end of the year she changed her title to MRS. E. H. STOWE M.D.

Other people now knew what to call Emily, but many still didn't know what to think of her. Some thought she must be an eccentric. Others saw her as an intellectual filled with knowledge. Some people thought she was crazy.

Augusta age 10, John Howard age 6, and Frank age 4 found it strange to have a mother as a doctor, the only one in Canada. Augusta loved to watch her mother and wanted to follow in her footsteps. Frank couldn't wait to climb aboard Emily's carriage and ride off to visit the patients. Those who could afford it liked the doctor to come to their homes.

Women Patients

Many women were glad to have a female doctor. Women were modest in Emily's time and often too shy to undress for a doctor's examination. They would suffer pain and infection rather than visit a male doctor.

Women's uncomfortable, impractical clothing caused medical problems. Long, bulky dresses made moving around difficult. Corsets pulled in their waists to 18 inches, squashing their internal organs. Emily had so many patients that she had to move several times into larger offices.

GIRLS' CLOTHES

A girl aged thirteen wore a stiff corset which squeezed her body into the fashionable shape. She also put on a corset cover, long drawers and five or six starched petticoats. Next she added a dress with a high neck, long sleeves and tight waist. Her full skirt swept the ground.

No Licence

BAD BLOOD – OLD MEDICINE

When Emily graduated in 1867, doctors believed disease came from bad blood. Drawing out the bad blood was considered the best treatment for every sickness. A visit from the doctor meant leeches for bloodletting. Sometimes the patient fainted. At the end of his visit, the doctor would often pull a tooth, or prescribe enemas and mineral waters.

Although Emily was in demand, legally she still wasn't a doctor. Why? In 1865 Canada passed a new law. To get a licence, every doctor who had studied in the United States had to take one session at a Canadian university. The problem was, Emily wasn't allowed into the university. So for the next 13 years Emily practised without a licence.

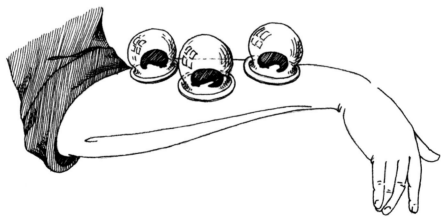

36

Alone

Once a patient of Emily's asked another doctor for his opinion. The doctor arrived, took off his coat and tall black hat, examined the patient and then met Emily in the front room.

The doctor said he was confused and had never seen a case like this before. He kept muttering, while pacing around the room.

Emily stared at him as he paced back and forth. The patient had the flu. There was nothing unusual. Why was this doctor so upset? He mumbled under his breath, then yelled out loud that this case was unsettling.

Finally, Emily understood. He wasn't concerned about the patient. He was upset about consulting with a woman doctor! Emily convinced him with her pleasant but firm manner that it was permissible to talk about the case with a woman.

Most male doctors felt the same way about discussing medicine with Emily. The profession stood aloof, distrustful of this new creature. Emily worked alone.

MEDICINES OF THE LAST CENTURY

Some regularly-used medicines, such as mercury and arsenic, we now know are poisons. Popular cough syrups of the time often contained addictive drugs. Dr. Ayer's Cherry Pectoral for colds contained heroin and Mrs. Winslow's Soothing Syrup had morphine. People thought the medicines worked because they made the patient feel good, but they did not cure anything.

No Complaints

JENNY TROUT

Like Emily, Jenny had lived on a farm and taught school. She and Emily were the first women to attend the Toronto School of Medicine. They sat in the medical amphitheatre listening to lectures and watching demonstrations. Together, they endured daily taunts and humiliation. Afterwards, Jenny went to the United States to become a doctor.

Jenny Trout, Emily's next door neighbour, was friendly and respected Emily's views. Although Jenny was ten years younger than forty-year old Emily, they became good friends and Jenny supported Emily's interest in women's rights and medicine. Together, they decided to try to go to medical college. Emily still hoped to become a licensed doctor.

Dr. William Thomas Aikins, president of the Toronto School of Medicine, arranged for the two women to attend lectures in 1871. The only requirement was that the women had to promise they would not complain about anything, no matter what happened.

Torment

EARLY OPERATIONS

Ether was first used in 1846. It put the patient to sleep, making amputations and operations much easier. Doctors operated in their street clothes without gloves or masks.

A great deal happened. The professors and students took part in a campaign to torment Emily and Jenny. Every day the two women took deep breaths and gave one another courage to face the bitter ridicule. Just walking to classes was an ordeal as people huddled in circles to watch and criticize. Even little children, playing in the street, stopped and pointed as they passed.

Bystanders assumed these women must either be bad or insane. Once inside, students laughed when the women asked questions. Parts of cadavers (dead bodies used for dissection) were left on their chairs. So much degrading graffiti was scribbled all over the school that the walls had to be painted with whitewash four times.

The men wanted to make Emily and Jenny miserable so that they would go home. Even some professors were cruel and urged the male students on. Emily encouraged Jenny to speak up. One day, when a lecturer told a joke about women, Jenny shot to her feet. She'd had enough! If he didn't stop, she warned him, she would inform his wife!

Things improved after that. The women managed to stay until the end of the course.

One of the first uses of anesthesia

39

Final Exam

OUT LOUD

The College of Physicians and Surgeons of Ontario conducted the exam. Each student sat with one examiner for 10 minutes. When the large bell in the hall rang, the students moved to the next examiner. At the end of the day, the student stood before all the professors while the results were announced as "favourable" or "unfavourable."

EMILY'S SCRAP BOOK.

Emily kept a scrap book. She cut out newspaper articles and pasted them into her book. Then she took a pen and put comments beside each article. One clipping in Emily's scrap book originally said, "Dr. Emily Stowe and her friend Mrs. Trout." After Emily and Jenny were no longer friends, Emily scratched out Jenny's name.

The exam was done partially out loud. The College of Physicians and Surgeons kept a record of Emily taking the exam in 1872 in the following subjects: botany, anatomy, chemistry, physiology, toxicology and materia medica. Botany, the science of plants, was the only subject in which Emily did well, getting a mark of 79. This mark was not enough and Emily did not pass her final exam.

Perhaps with three children and a busy practice, she didn't have enough time to study. Maybe the questions were about traditional, not homeopathic medicine, or perhaps the examiners deliberately made it difficult for her.

In any case, Emily quickly put this failure behind her. So, still without a licence, she went back to her busy practice. Jenny made plans to study medicine in the United States.

By the time Jenny came back from the U.S. as a doctor, she and Emily were no longer friends. For uncertain reasons they became competitors.

Perhaps Emily didn't like Jenny asserting herself as a traditional, not homeopathic, physician. Emily probably didn't take kindly to Jenny's returning to Toronto, passing her exam and receiving her medical licence.

Jenny Trout became Canada's first *licensed* woman doctor.

DO YOU HAVE DROPSY?

On her exam Emily had to answer the following question: "Define the term *Dropsy*. State the various causes that lead to it in the acute and chronic form." This sickness called Dropsy was invented to explain many illnesses. An advertisement in 1873 asked: "Do your feet swell at night? Are your eyelids puffy? Do you feel a general stiffness about your flesh? In a word you have the early symptoms of *Dropsy*. If so, let us advise you to use Wilson's Tonic."

Electric Medicine

Jenny moved away from Emily's neighbourhood and set up an expensive, large electric-treatment centre. From 1877 to 1882, she ran The Therapeutic and Electrical Institute in Toronto. In the late 1800's, many doctors believed that electricity cured everything.

An electric belt was supposed to stop stomach troubles. One salesman applied electricity to soap and came up with Dingman's Electric Soap. Emily continued to treat her patients with homeopathy.

A HOLE IN HIS STOMACH

In the early 1800's, a man was wounded by a shot that blasted a hole into his stomach. A doctor was able to study how the stomach worked by looking through this freak hole. This doctor wrote the first book about the stomach and how it used gastric juices to break down food.

Emily impressed everybody at the trial.

On Trial

In 1879, a domestic servant, Sarah Ann Lovell, came to Emily's office. Emily gave her a homeopathic medicine. Something went wrong and the girl died. Emily went to court to stand trial.

Emily's enemies thought this problem proved that women shouldn't be doctors. They complained that all Emily did was visit and have tea with rich women. If women wanted to be doctors, they should just deliver babies or help male doctors.

Emily remembered her great-uncle and how he had gone to jail for his beliefs. With her strong, confident voice, she defended herself, explaining that the girl's death had nothing to do with her homeopathic medicine.

During the trial, Emily spoke about her remedies, her practice and the people she had cured. Other physicians listened and were impressed with her knowledge. Perhaps, for the first time, they saw beyond Emily being a woman and viewed her as a real doctor, knowledgeable and caring. Finally, Emily was found not guilty.

Emily won the respect of other doctors who had followed the trial. Although she had already been practising medicine for 13 years, the College of Physicians and Surgeons of Ontario, soon after the trial, allowed Emily to become a member. On July 16, 1880, Emily Stowe, at the age of 49, received her medical licence.

HEROIC MEDICINE

Medicine in Emily's time was sometimes called heroic medicine. Here is an example of what was done to a man who had cholera:

"He was bled thirty ounces, given 15 grains of calomel and two of opium, given a turpentine enema, rubbed with turpentine for his cramps, and then given ginger tea.

Later the same day he had 3 grains of calomel, 1/8 grain of opium every half-hour with calomel every third hour.

In the evening he was dosed with castor oil.

The next day he was given an enema and dosed with calomel, opium, castor oil and port wine every two or three hours.

The next day he was dosed with rhubarb, had twelve leeches applied to his stomach. Then he was given beef tea and arrowroot. By this time the mercury had begun to blister his mouth."

It is no wonder this type of medicine was called heroic. The patient had to be a hero to withstand the treatment.

Infections

Doctors were desperately trying to understand disease. How could a simple scratch lead to infection and even death?

The connection between germs and sickness wasn't understood. People didn't wash their hands or take baths regularly. Doctors operated in their street clothes, using instruments that weren't sterile. Doctors went from dissecting dead bodies to operating on patients without washing their hands. This led to many problems, especially infections. Often the patient was covered in pus.

Doctors kept testing new methods like the electric machines that Jenny used. Then two major discoveries changed medicine forever.

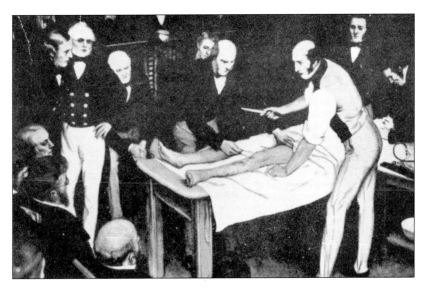

Joseph Lister, standing at the left, watching an operation in 1846.

Germs

CARBOLIC SPRAY

Carbolic acid had already been used to clean sewers. Joseph Lister decided to dilute it, making the acid thinner, and use it during operations. This spray, known as phenol, killed the germs on cuts and wounds. This was the beginning of antiseptics. Carbolic spray stopped infections and saved thousands of lives.

A cartoon made fun of the germ idea. How could all these livng things exist in one drop of water?

In 1855, a French doctor, Louis Pasteur, saw tiny living things called microbes under a microscope. He called them germs. He proved that these germs lived everywhere, even in air and water, but no one could see them.

Then in 1865, another doctor, Lord Joseph Lister, read about these germs. He thought about the infections that set in after surgery. Maybe these germs were on the surgeons' dirty hands and scalpels. Lister developed a "carbolic spray" to kill the germs during an operation. At first, doctors made fun of Lister, just as they did of Emily and her new ideas. When they finally tried Lister's spray, doctors used too much and wet everything. One doctor had to wear boots during his operations because he flooded the floor.

Lister struggled for twelve years to convince other doctors that his spray would save lives. Gradually, people started to believe in germs. Once people washed regularly and once doctors accepted Lister's spray, the world of medicine changed. Fewer people got sick. Infections decreased. By 1877, doctors wore white coats, used gloves and sterilized equipment.

Emily followed all these changes. She taught her patients about the importance of germs and washing.

The Secret Club

HOW TO BE A GOOD MOTHER

One of the club members, Mrs. Sarah Ann Curzon, presented a paper on parenting. This is what she wrote in 1880:

1. Parents should never shift their own responsibility towards their children on to teachers or pastors.

2. Parents should be careful to provide sound reading for their children from their earliest years.

3. Provide your children with innocent mental recreation of their quiet moments.

4. Never taunt your children: neither with their faults, their shortcomings, nor their physical or mental defects.

By 1876, Emily's carriage was a familiar sight on the streets of Toronto. Even though her practice kept her busy visiting patients, she had not forgotten her encounter with John McCaul, the President of the University of Toronto, and her promise to help other women. Emily knew now that, by herself, she couldn't change the pattern of women's lives. She needed a group of like-minded women who were courageous enough to fight for women's rights.

Remembering her friends in the U.S. and how the newspapers had slandered them, Emily was careful about naming this new group. She called it The Toronto Women's Literary Club, so that people would think they were talking about books. Actually, the members used their meetings to give lectures on important, controversial issues.

Emily talked about giving girls choices and changing the patterns of their lives. Girls were smart enough to have a university education. Capable women could take part in politics.

Emily said: "We should not just watch what is going on politically. It's like trying to learn to swim by watching a frog in a basin. If we want to learn to swim, we must get in the water ourselves. We must be a part of the political life of our country."

A cartoon poster in the late 1800s

POLITICS

Women were not allowed to vote or run for political office. Although there were many women teachers, the women had to sit quietly at teachers' meetings. Emily fought for women's right to voice their opinions. She wanted women to vote. Emily believed women should be able to become politicians and help to make new laws.

No Woman, Idiot, Lunatic or Criminal

Soon the women saw the vote as their most important goal. Canada's law stated, "No woman, idiot, lunatic or criminal shall vote." Emily and The Literary Club wanted to change the law. They thought that once they could vote, they would be able to change the other unfair laws. So, in 1883, they renamed the club The Toronto Women's Suffrage Association.

Most people thought these women should go back home and be quiet. Even Emily's family found it, at times, embarrassing. No other family had a woman like Emily, a doctor and now a suffragist.

One of Emily's friends explained that young people didn't like to feel different. Emily's niece didn't mind. She said that, although Emily was different, she was "fair-minded and charitable" and that her "trail-blazing" was not just for herself but for the sake of all Canadian women.

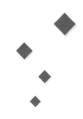

John Returns

TOADS AND TEETH

The skin of toads, dried and powdered, was used for toothaches and bleeding gums.

Emily's husband John never complained about these meetings. After returning to the family in 1873, he apprenticed to become a dentist. There was no school for dentistry, so he trained with a dentist, learning while helping.

Then, when John became a dentist, the Stowes moved into a larger house and set up a joint practice. The children could always find their father at home or in his adjoining office. Emily, their mother, was usually visiting patients or attending meetings.

John encouraged Emily in all her new endeavours. She did not have to convince him that gaining women's rights was a worthy cause. But how could Emily change the minds of other people who insisted that the pattern stay the same?

WOMEN CAN'T VOTE

People who were against women voting believed females were not smart enough. They thought it would destroy the family, with the wife voting for one party and her husband for another. Some said that allowing women to vote was against the teachings of the Bible. Cartoons suggested that intelligent women had large foreheads. Emily said that these people could not separate themselves from the "habits and thoughts that traditions had given them."

Allan Gardens, Toronto

Let's Pretend

Emily had an idea. If the male-female roles could be reversed, then the laws would look ridiculous.

Emily set up a mock parliament. Run by women pretending to be in power politically, a meeting was held to discuss whether or not men should vote. Newspaper reporters hovered around Allan Gardens on February 18, 1896, writing down every word Emily said as she played the part of the Attorney-General.

They called themselves the Ontario Legislature of Women and acted out a meeting with a pretend delegation of men who were asking for the vote.

Emily rose. The audience was silent. Emily said that although she personally thought men should receive the vote she did not wish to give them false hope. She explained that the members of her cabinet who were forward-thinking, bright women, could somehow not agree with her.

If they gave men the vote, soon men would want to wear women's clothes and do women's work. This would upset everything. Men should do the domestic work and leave the running of the country to women.

The delegation of men went away unhappy.

'Very intelligent women are seldom beautiful, their features, and particularly their foreheads are more or less masculine'

Magazine Cartoon 1892

Heaps of Fun

THE FIRST TIME

In 1887, Emily's club drew up the first voting petition to take to the Canadian government. Emily went door-to-door for signatures. Some women slammed the door in Emily's face.

A FRIEND IN PARLIAMENT

Mr. John Waters, Liberal member of the Ontario Legislature, raised the question of women voting in each session for eight years. The other members laughed loudly every time.

SMOKING

Smoking was considered a man's activity. Men used pipes freely in public, but women were embarrassed to smoke.

Then the women discussed how the men had looked. It was decided that they were peculiar, their gowns ugly and their hairstyles out of date. These men who wanted the vote were a cheap imitation of real men who understood their place. Anyone could see by their strong bodies that they were meant for physical labour, not intellectual pursuits.

Then these women on the pretend legislature suggested other measures, such as the ringing of a curfew bell at 10 o'clock each evening, warning all men off the streets unless accompanied by their wives. Another member recommended the invention of a special pipe designed so that the smoker consumed his own smoke.

Emily and her mock parliament decided not to give the vote to men. Of course, when it was all over, they laughed. The next day the newspapers said the Women's Parliament was amusing and afforded "heaps of fun."

The women hoped that, despite the laughter, some people understood the serious message.

Emily's Club Wins

Gradually, more and more people did begin to understand. Still, Emily's goals of higher education and the vote for Canadian women would take much longer than she'd hoped. Changing the way people thought was a slow process.

Meanwhile, Emily's club fought for smaller, but important things, like better working conditions for women and children. In the new factories and "sweatshops," young girls often worked 10 – 12 hours a day. Emily's group was able to supply them with chairs and separate bathrooms. They helped pass the Factory Act in 1886 that made it illegal in Ontario to hire females under fourteen and males under twelve.

PUBLIC HEALTH

As Toronto became larger, so did the problems with cleanliness and health. There were no inspectors for meat and milk. Sewage and waste, even slaughterhouse remains, were dumped into the Toronto Harbour and then city water was piped to homes. Garbage was dumped in back lanes. Emily's club fought for a permanent Board of Health to keep the city clean and safe.

Special Success

Emily's group continually sent petitions asking for women to be allowed into the University of Toronto. Repeatedly, they helped women mail applications. Over and over again, women were rejected.

After many years, some men started to see things differently. Women like Emily had proven that girls could learn university subjects. Still, women were turned down because now many male leaders thought there should be separate universities, but there wasn't enough money for another school.

Finally, as a result of Emily's perseverance, women were accepted into the University of Toronto. Women students walked through those large doors in the 1884 session. This was a very special success for Emily.

Professor John McCaul had retired, but he was shocked to see Emily's prediction come true, as women entered the University of Toronto. Over twenty years had passed since their meeting, but Emily had kept her promise.

UNIVERSITY WOMEN

Most people agreed with John McCaul, president of the University of Toronto, that women weren't smart enough for university. Emily had to prove that women could learn university subjects.

Augusta Stowe,
Emily's daughter

STRIKE

In 1880, Queens University in Kingston, Ontario permitted a few women to enter its medical program. The male students went on strike, threatening to go to another university. The women were asked to leave. One of the women students said the whole experience was like going through a "fiery furnace."

Not A Path Of Roses

Another triumph for Emily was her daughter Augusta's graduation in 1883 from Victoria College Medical School. Augusta was the first woman to obtain her medical degree in Canada.

It wasn't easy. After listening to rude jokes, ridicule and laughter, she would often cry all the way home. When she graduated, Augusta said, "The first pioneer woman to study medicine in Canada had not a pathway strewn with roses."

Her daughter's experience convinced Emily that women needed a separate medical college. Emily gathered about 40 people to plan a college for women. Jenny Trout came, assuming her donation of $10,000.00 meant that she could set the rules for this new school. Emily disagreed. Jenny took her money to Kingston where Queen's University accepted her offer for a new college.

Meanwhile, Emily continued to work towards a new school in Toronto. On October 1, 1883, The Woman's Medical College officially opened. The rented house at 289 Sumach Street was often called the medical "cottage." In Kingston, exactly one day later, Jenny opened her college, but it only lasted a few years.

Emily's school continued to grow, changing its name to the Ontario Medical College for Women. This became The Women's College Hospital. The word "College" remained to honour Emily and her original idea.

Retirement

Even after John died in 1891, Emily continued to work. Then, in 1893, when she was 62 years-old, she retired from medical practice. She still lectured and worked for the club which was now called Dominion Women's Enfranchisement Association.

Many people came to hear Emily speak. Some wanted to see what a woman doctor looked like. They wondered if she looked like a man, but what they saw was an attractive older woman, speaking strongly about her beliefs. She talked about women being capable. She spoke about justice and fairness for women and men. She mentioned equal education and choice of careers. Then she talked about voting and health. Many listened and slowly people started to agree.

Struggling for women's rights meant changing the way people viewed women. It involved years and years of organizing petitions, writing the government, attending meetings and giving lectures.

53

EMILY SPEAKS

When Emily first started making speeches, the audience was against her and she could feel their intense dislike. But things changed by 1896 and newspapers said she looked like a picture with her white hair and black silk gown. Emily spoke like an actor, letting her voice rise and fall. She leaned heavily on her cane as people listened with respect and admiration.

Accident

In 1893, while speaking at the World's Fair in Chicago, Emily fell off the stage and hurt her leg. After the accident, she walked with a cane and often went to rest in Muskoka.

She enjoyed the quiet of her own cottage on a small island she named Stowe Island. She planted a garden that reminded her of Hannah and her youth. Once again, she lived in the country surrounded by her beloved plants and fragrances.

Somehow, she still managed to lead the women's group. She led them to victory after victory as women gained education, property and political rights.

The President of the Women's Historical Society at that time stated, "It was from the doctor's (Emily's) liberal views that all the progress made by women in this province (Ontario) particularly and the others incidentally sprang."

All women living in Canada benefited from Emily's work.

Piece by Piece

CREMATION

Emily wanted to be cremated when she died.

"I have never done an act upon earth to pollute it, and I do not wish to do so in dissolution." There was no crematorium in Toronto. Her body was taken to Buffalo and then the ashes were brought back to Toronto.

Emily assumed that people would not agree with her new and different ideas. She understood that the struggle for women's rights meant that she would be insulted and criticized.

Emily said: "My life was one of much struggle characterized by the usual persecution which attends everyone who pioneers a movement or steps out of line with established custom."

This great person, whose work still affects Canada, passed away on April 30, 1903, one day before her seventy-second birthday. For five decades, she had fought for her belief that girls should have the right to design their own future. She had helped them add pattern pieces to their lives, but the work was not complete.

Like an unfinished quilt, women's lives were still missing many pieces. Augusta, Emily's daughter, continued the long struggle for equality.

WHENEVER
by Sydell Waxman

Whenever
  a woman votes,
  a girl dreams
  of a career,
Whenever
  she becomes
  what she chooses
  to be,
Whenever
  a politician is female,
  or she graduates
  from university,

We should pause.

Think back to Emily
Remember how a girl
Busy on a farm
Learned to teach and heal
Learned to respect herself
And other women's
capabilities
  enough
  to fight
  a nation.

A Personal Pattern

Emily Stowe envisioned a different society. Many of the changes she started are still developing.

Just as she had promised, women entered the University of Toronto. Emily made it possible for women to study and become doctors in Canada.

She set up the first women's medical school, which became The Women's College Hospital in Toronto. She educated people about germs, homeopathic healing and about women's capabilities and rights.

Emily started the Canadian women's movement and fought for the vote for women.

Emily's greatest wish came true fourteen years after she died. In 1917, Canadian women finally won the federal right to vote.

Canadian girls today have a choice of futures and can create their own life patterns. They can go to university. They can vote. They can choose careers. Emily Howard Stowe M.D. made it happen. She forged a personal pattern for her own life and gave others the power to create their own design.

56

CANADA HONOURS EMILY

Bronze Bust at Toronto City Hall
Canadian Stamp, March 1981
Picture in Women's College Hospital
Emily Stowe Shelter for Women
Dr. Emily Stowe Public School

IMPORTANT DATES

1831 Emily Howard Jennings is born.
1832 Chloroform is used to help patients during operations.
1846 Ether is used for the first time to put patients to sleep.
1849 Elizabeth Blackwell graduates as the first woman doctor in the United States.
1850 The first Women's Medical College in Philadelphia, Pennsylvania opens with the support of the Quakers.
1859 An act "Respecting Homeopathy" is passed and homeopathic doctors receive licences.
1863 Dr. Clemence Sophia Lozier opens the New York Medical College for Women. Later, Emily attends this school.
1867 Dr. Emily Stowe becomes Canada's first woman doctor.
1875 Jenny Trout becomes first licensed woman physician in Canada.
1875 John Stowe finishes his apprenticeship and becomes a dentist.
1877 Emily organizes The Toronto Women's Literary Club.
1877 Antiseptic methods used for medicine. Doctors begin to wear white gowns.
1879 Emily Stowe is put on trial.
1880 On July 1, Emily receives her licence as a Canadian doctor. She becomes a member of the College of Physicians and Surgeons.
1883 Emily's club changes its name to The Toronto Women's Suffrage Association.
1883 Sir John A. Macdonald introduces the first three suffrage bills. All three are defeated.
1883 Augusta, Emily's daughter, graduates as the first woman to obtain a medical degree in Canada.
1883 Ontario Medical College for Women is established.
1884 The University of Toronto admits women.
1889 Emily's club becomes Dominion Women's Enfranchisement Association.
1891 John Stowe dies.
1893 Emily Stowe retires from her medical practice.
1893 The National Council of Women is formed.
1896 A mock parliament is organized and run by Emily.
1903 Emily Howard Stowe dies.
1916 Women in Alberta, Saskatchewan and Manitoba receive the provincial vote.
1917 Women in British Columbia and Ontario receive the right to vote. Women are given full-federal franchise.

SYDELL WAXMAN

Sydell Blossom Waxman, a former teacher-librarian, has published magazine articles in Canada and the United States. Recently, her work was selected for the anthology *Far and Wide*. Sydell has lectured on *Women of the Last Century* at museums in the Toronto area. *Changing the Pattern* is the culmination of years of research into Sydell's favourite topics, history and children's books. Currently, she writes children's books while teaching *Creative Writing* and *Writing for Children* in Toronto. Sydell lives in Thornhill with her husband Allan and children Julie, Kyle and Adlai.

The author is indebted to the following people for their time and knowledge:
Barbara Greenwood, author
Lisa Miettinen, archivist, Norwich archives
Mary Gladwin, archivist, Norwich archives
Joan Mitchell, Wilfrid Laurier University Archives/Library
Sarah Montgomery, National Archives
Jon Schmitz, archivist, College of Physicians and Surgeons of Ontario

Sources of research:
Academy of Medicine Collection
Archives of College of Physicians and Surgeons
City of Toronto Archives
Emily Stowe papers at Wilfrid Laurier University
Hannah Institute
Metropolitan Toronto Reference Library
Norwich Archives
Ontario Archives
Religious Society of Friends Library
Stowe and Stowe-Gullen papers at Victoria University
Thomas Fisher Rare Book Library, University of Toronto
Women's College Hospital Library
Women's Resource Centre, O.I.S.E.

PICTURE CREDITS